The Five Needs of Every Teenager

Become the Kind of Adult Every Young Person Wants To Talk To

———————

By: Shawn M. McBride

The Five Needs of Every Teenager

Copyright © 2017 by Shawn Maurice McBride

All rights reserved. No part of this book may be reproduced or transmitted in any form or by any means without written permission from the author.

ISBN-13:978-1548093532

ISBN-10: 154809353X

Dedication

This book is dedicated to Dr. Bernard T. Fuller, the Founder and Senior Pastor of New Song Bible Fellowship Church in Lanham, MD. In the Fall of 1997, Pastor Fuller afforded me my first opportunity to work full time in youth ministry. It was very rare for a church minister to get paid a salary, benefits and a budget to serve kids back then. His confidence in me allowed me to be completely focused on serving students in middle and high school over a three-year period. His wise guidance and good leadership during that time was extremely meaningful and encouraging to me as a young 23-year-old kid with a wife and very young children of my own. Little did I know that the hands-on experience I gleaned while working with teenagers in that community would literally became the foundation for this book project years later.

"Young people don't care how much you know until they know how much you really care." - **Josh McDowell** in *Youth Ministry Handbook: Making the Connection*

Introduction

Over the last 25 years I have given my life to helping teenagers and their families. Serving teenagers has been my life's calling. It's hard for me to believe that I have been so fortunate by the Lord's grace to serve literally hundreds of thousands of kids through speaking, mentoring, emailing, writing, texting and face-to-face counseling. More importantly, I am super blessed to be the father of five remarkable and outstanding children who regularly teach and help me to become a better father. At the time of this writing my children are ages 27, 18, 17, 15 and almost 12. Pray for your boy!

My specific purpose for writing this book is to share with you five crucial principles I have learned over the past 25 years as a parent, mentor and pastor as it relates to understanding and engaging teenagers relationally and emotionally. The operative words are RELATIONALLY and EMOTIONALLY.

The Transitional Years Ages 13-19

The adolescent years are ones of transition. Our teenagers are struggling to become independent, even as they quietly cling to the security of dependence. They can literally feel themselves changing, both emotionally and physically, and are sometimes overwhelmed with the conflicts they feel raging within. They aren't nearly as convinced of the normalcy of all this turbulence as we are.

Teens are also experiencing innumerable pressures, including pressures to succeed, please others and themselves, do what they want to do and be whom they want to be, all while worrying about fitting in and being accepted. No wonder they're so moody. We would be too.

Who is this Book For?

This book is for you if you are seeking to have a better relationship with a teenager you are parenting, mentoring, teaching or investing your time in their life in any capacity.

The principles that I will share with you are universal regardless of the ethnicity or age group of a young person. Once learned and practiced, these principles will become the catalyst for transforming your relationship with the teenagers in your life.

I can assure you that these principles will bring it

all together and enable you to have a greater impact in the lives of the teens most important to you, regardless of whether you are a parent, teacher, caring adult volunteer in your church or mentor.

Shawn McBride, Washington DC Summer 2017

Table of Contents

Introduction 6

Chapter 1: *Teenagers Need Your Quality Time* 10

Chapter 2: *Teenagers Need Sincere Appreciation* 27

Chapter 3: *Teenagers Need Honest Affection* 45

Chapter 4: *Teenagers Need Unconditional Acceptance* 63

Chapter 5: *Teenagers Need Consistent Accountability* 81

Relational Youth Ministry 100

Chapter 1: Teenagers Need Your Quality Time

Perhaps one of the most important and yet most difficult part of ourselves to give our teens is our time. Today's world is hectic. It's chaotic. It's exhausting.

And although parents and those of us who work with teens know we need to be available, we often find ourselves exploring the alternatives. Because we are so busy, we try to get away with sending in the B team: We give them money, we make sure they have the basic necessities of life, we provide the cell phone. We work hard to ensure they have a roof over their heads and clean clothes to wear. We give them everything we have except what they really need, which is a piece of ourselves.

Although they might argue differently, it's truly not the stuff that teenagers need. Those of us who work with them understand that they need us. They need our time. They need our attention. They need for us to be available for them in a determined, intentional and focused way. Most kids that I have met and served over the years spell love this way: T.I.M.E. This means that young people measure love by the T.I.M.E and attention that we give to them. This is far different than how most adults spell love.

Absentee Parents

Spending quality time with young people is difficult for most parents and adults mainly because of the various demands on our lives and schedules each and every day. Many of today's teens are living with what many call absentee parents. Sure, the parents love their children, but because their own lives are chaotic, they are not always present for their teens in the way that's needed. If you are a person who works with teens, you cannot completely make up for an absentee parent. What you can do, however, is be there in a capacity of support. You can show your teens how much you care. You can speak to them and listen to them about their concerns, and you can provide the guidance and wisdom they may not be getting at home. It's an essential role, and it is yours for the taking.

Reasons to Be Available: Greater Success

One of the many lessons I have learned in my research for this writing project is that teens who have adult involvement in their lives are more successful. It's as plain and simple as that. Research demonstrates that they are less likely to engage in risky behaviors, they tend to get better grades, they pursue higher degrees of education and they are overall happier and more emotionally balanced. I was amazed to learn that teens who have engaged adults in their lives are far more likely to be successful in school and in life. They not only graduate from high school at a higher rate, but they are also more likely to pursue higher education. When they have the support of committed adults who want to see them become successful, who can and do espouse the importance of education, and who can and do discuss and even monitor their educational progress, they rise to the expectations laid out for them. There's plenty of evidence to convince us that we must slow down and become more available for our teens. Being there for your teens, being present and available in a focused, intentional way, can quickly determine the behaviors that can, without being overly dramatic, save or destroy them.

Reasons to Be Available: Their Emotional Well-Being

Teens who have parents and caring adults actively available are more likely to be emotionally healthy and strong. It is the notion of being actively available that is so important. It isn't good enough to promise to make yourself available if they need you. You must be available as much as possible. They must come to trust that you'll be there - even when they aren't sure they want you.

Yes, this is difficult. Yes, it can be time-consuming and emotionally draining. But if you love the teens with whom are your own offspring and those you work with, you must be present in a focused way.

You must be available when they need to talk. You must be there to support them when they are down. You must be there as a role model cheerleader, mentor, advisor and friend. You must be there to cushion the inevitable falls as they make their way from childhood to adulthood.

Teens who have the benefit of this adult involvement in their lives are engaged in the process of growing and learning in a less chaotic, less hit-or-miss fashion. They have more self-confidence and a higher sense of purpose - all of which translates into a stronger sense of self and a healthier emotional outlook.

Reasons to Be Available: Their Self Esteem

Teens who have adult availability in their lives have much higher self-esteem than those who cannot count on regular and/or genuine adult involvement. They are quicker to develop stronger self-control and are better able to manage the frustrations, confusions and disappointments that persist throughout the teenage years. When these kids have adults who are intentional in their presence, when they have the love, availability and responsiveness of loving adults, their psychological development is stronger and smoother. They develop the self-confidence needed to navigate through the emotional turmoil of their teenage years much more successfully.

Reasons to Be Available: Less Stress

Teens who have adults around them that consistently show interest in their lives and regularly discuss - in a non-judgmental, non-accusatory way - the importance of socially-acceptable behavior, exhibit fewer signs of aggression and have fewer behavioral issues. They experience less anxiety and depression. The more these caring adults are involved, the more they talk with their teens. They pay attention to what their teens are doing and with whom, and they are actively involved in their teens' activities. The more involved parents and caring adults are, the more successfully teens learn to manage their own behaviors.

Reasons to Be Available: Less Delinquency

Teenagers who have the support and affection of parents and caring adults engage in anti-social and/or delinquent behaviors less often. When our teenagers know they are being supervised and, when they know they have an adult in their lives who cares enough to pay attention, they are far less likely to bow to any peer pressure they may encounter. They have the courage and insight to keep themselves out of trouble. They have a greater respect for themselves and a greater sense of right and wrong. They feel more connected to society and have a greater respect for the law.

Reasons to Be Available: Less Self-Medication

Teens who have an involved adult consistently present in their lives do not succumb to substance use and abuse nearly as often as those who do not. Studies have shown that your teens are far less likely to smoke tobacco, drink alcohol and/or experiment with drugs when you are actively available and your focus is on being there for the teens in your charge.

Teens equate your focused availability with higher expectations and they respond by placing higher expectations on themselves. They understand that such high-risk behaviors can be deterrents to their success, and, therefore, are more likely to abstain.

Reasons to Be Available: Higher Standards & Performance

Overall, teenagers who have adults involved in their lives achieve to higher standards. Doing simple activities with the teens in your charge and spending quality time with them leads to better performance in school. They equate your involvement with a concern for their overall performance and success. They work harder, learn more, care more and get better grades. Going to the movies, attending sporting events, going out for breakfast, lunch or dinner, spending time just chatting about their lives, their interests and their concerns gives them a reason to do well. They want to please you and they want to succeed in whatever they do. Helping them with homework, talking about their dreams and exploring their goals: all of these types of interactions translates into a focused availability that allows teens to be more successful in school and, ultimately, in life.

How to Be Available

So how exactly are you to express to your teens that you are, indeed, available? How do you make sure they know that you care and that you are available to meet their emotional needs? How, exactly, are you to let them know that they can trust you, that they can count on you to not only be their leader, but an adult who sincerely and genuinely cares for them?

Be Present

There are so, so many ways. Always and most importantly, you show them you are available through your intentionally consistent presence. You show them through your words, your actions and your interactions. You show them through the joy you receive in sharing in their lives.

Be A Model

Setting an example for your teens is a way of being there for them. It's truly as important as paying attention. When they see that you are kind and decent and care about them as individuals, they will admire and respect you. They will want to emulate you. They will understand that you are there to help them grow, which is what being available is all about.

Remember that your teens are always watching. They are waiting to catch you not caring. They are waiting to have their hopes and expectations dashed once again by an adult who didn't do what they said they would do. They are waiting to be let down once again. However, when you do what you say you will do; when you are there when you say you'll be there, your teens will quickly learn that you are sincere.

They will come to trust you. They will come to rely on you being available. And that is when they will open up to you. That is when you can begin to be truly effective and impact their lives.

Set Expectations

One of the most important aspects of working with children and teens is to provide them with safety. Although teens will talk big talk about how grown up they are, how independent they are and how they rely on no one, they want to be loved and they want to feel safe. We all do. Part of being available for your teen is by being available to give them the security they need.

The best way to keep your teens safe, from themselves and from others, is to outline your expectations. Consider as you do so to include them in determining what those expectations of behavior should be. Setting forth both rules and requirements helps teenagers know for sure what is and is not acceptable. It helps them develop into caring, responsible adults, and, ultimately, into responsible and contributing members of society.

Show Them That You Care

Your teens, from the petite, little 5' eighth-grade girl to the 6'3", 200 lb. sophomore boy, need your love. They need to know that you care and are there for them. With a smile or a wink or a pat on the back, they must know that they matter to you. Showing how much you care for them helps them to understand that they are deserving of your affection and attention. Even those teens with whom you work who keep you at arm's length will warm to your affection if you keep it light and unintimidating.

Help Them Set Goals

Our teens are very caught up in today. Today, after all, is their whole world. Today is when and where their friends live. Today is when and where both their concerns and their triumphs live. For our teens, it's all about today.

Helping your teens set goals gets them out of the limits of today. It allows them to think beyond this sometimes troublesome present of their lives toward what might be an exciting, successful future. Having you right there with them as they plan gives them the nudge they need to work to make it happen. It tells them that you care not only about who they are right now, but about who they will become. It's a way to extend your focused availability past their present needs and far into their futures. Once they get there, they will look back and thank you.

Be the Adult

We have established that working with teens can be difficult. There are times when, although you've done everything in your power to be there for them and to show them that you genuinely care and are available when they need, that you make decisions they resist. At times, that resistance can be quite noisy. At other times, that resistance can be downright rebellious. But remember, you are the adult. You are wiser and more experienced.

That doesn't mean you should flaunt your age-earned esteem or belittle their youth. It does mean that with calm reason, you will sometimes have to work to convince these teens that you're the adult and they are the teenagers. Sometimes what you say goes. Plain and simple. But if you're always aware of their needs and sensitivities of which there are so many, and if you treat them fairly and with respect, they will come around. They may not like it, but they will return your sense of fairness and respect, and they will come around.

When Teens Need You the Most

Understand that the teens with whom you parent and work always need you. They may not know it and they certainly may not admit it. But, you must know it even when they don't.

There will be times when a teen needs you even more. Because their lives are so uncertain, because today they are dealing with more issues than any previous generation of teens has had to deal with, it is more important than ever that you be aware of their calls for help.

As you get to know your teens as individuals, you will know who they are and how they typically behave. You will know their attitudes and their moods. As you continue to develop a closer, more caring relationship, and as you work to create a stronger bond, you should watch for any signs that they are struggling. It is then that they will need you most.

The Warning Signs of Struggle: Pay Attention!

- They withdraw from you and from their peers.
- They seem agitated or restless.
- Their grades and/or school attendance suddenly begin to suffer.
- They become depressed for long periods of time.
- They erupt in anger easily.
- They appear less motivated and express fatigue and/or a lack of energy.
- Their group of friends change.
- They begin to speak of suicide.
- You either notice or hear that they are engaged in self-destructive behavior.

How to Answer the Call for Help

Keeping the lines of communication open and remaining available, even when they are adamant that they are fine and don't need you, is essential. You cannot assume they'll be fine. The sooner you identify a problem and work to help your teen deal with it, the more likely you'll be successful in helping him overcome whatever it is. Being there, being available to talk and to listen and to call in the experts when necessary, is vital in helping your teens navigate through this time in their lives when they need you more than ever.

I simply cannot stress enough that you must be there. You have to show up and be present in their lives. Be willing to talk and be willing to listen. Be interested in what they do. Care about what they care about. Tell them what you care about and share your interests with them.

And if they indicate that they really need you, even if you're in the middle of planning the next big event, set aside what you are doing and take a minute to pay attention. You'll know soon enough if it's important. If it is, put what you're doing aside and focus on what needs to be done.

Chapter 1 Questions for Reflection/Discussion

1. Being available in a focused way is not always easy for those of us who work with teens, especially

if we see them only once or so a week. Brainstorm a variety of ways that you can be intentionally available. What specific things can you say and do? What activities, programs, forums, etc. might you institute to make sure you are available for them in the focused way you intend?

2. Envision a group of teens that you've worked with for some time. You've established what you believe to be a strong and trusting relationship. Suddenly, however, you begin to sense that something in that relationship has gotten off kilter. Several of your teens are giving you a cold shoulder. They suddenly are no longer open to your attempts to communicate with them at a more personal level. What might you do?

3. Consider and discuss different ways you might impact your teens' efforts at school. What types of weekly activities might you begin as a way to help them value their education more and even perform better in their classes?

4. Imagine that one of your teens comes to you and tells you another teen in your group has been cutting herself. How might you handle this situation?

Chapter 2: Teenagers Need Sincere Appreciation

Mark Twain, known for his great stories, fun-loving sense of humor and witticisms once said, *"I could live for two months on a compliment."*

Couldn't we all? Teens are no different. There's nothing quite as nice as a compliment. There's nothing that makes us smile like a little sincere appreciation. We all need to know that we are valued. We all want to know we are recognized. Today's teens need that recognition, that appreciation, more than ever before.

Those of us who are lucky enough to work with teenagers must find ways to show how much we enjoy it. We must find ways to show our teens that we truly care, that we appreciate who they are and that we are so very glad they are in our lives.

Sincere appreciation helps to grow a teen's confidence and self-esteem, two of the most vital indicators of future success. When our teens know that we see their value, they begin to see their own. And isn't that why we are here? We're here to help these teens we love develop into the strong, confident and self-reliant individuals they were meant to be. We can do that. All it takes is a little sincere appreciation.

A Cure for Teen Alienation

So many of today's teens feel a profound sense of alienation. More than ever before, they are living lives of uncertainty. For many, their families, their schools and their societies are in a state of meltdown. They don't know where to turn. They end up isolating themselves from the chaos, often turning their backs on any support to which they might have access.

Because the teen years are a time of introspection and self-discovery, some of this alienation is normal. That, however, doesn't make it any easier for them to bear. Feelings of alienation, whether self-imposed or created by the struggles of their environment, leave many teens lonely, sometimes bordering on despair.

As you get to know your teens, one of the best things you can do to ease their troubles is to show them how much you truly appreciate each and every one of them. With appreciation, encouragement and open communication, you can positively impact their lives. You can begin to draw them out of the alienation that isolates them and welcome them to rejoin a world they can begin to see as a loving and accepting place.

Welcome to the World

As you welcome them back into the world, encourage them to talk. About anything. The teenage years can be moody, and we all know that teens can be melodramatic to a fault. With wild eyes and flailing arms, they will tell you of all the impositions they had to endure throughout their day. However much you want to smile at their histrionics, don't. You must take their struggles seriously, because their struggles are serious to them.

If you encourage your teen to talk about his struggles, if you let him vent his frustrations and fears, he will begin to come out of that self-imposed isolation. He will begin to see that you appreciate his concerns and insecurities as valid. So many people dismiss the trials of teenagers as trivial. Remember, these struggles are not at all trivial to your teen. Right now, this moment, is his life. It's important.

You might even share some of the struggles of your youth. After all, it hasn't been that long ago. With only a little effort, we can all remember how difficult it was to be a teenager. If you openly share in discussions and let them learn who you are, if you share what your hopes and dreams were and continue to be, they will begin to see that you trust and respect them. That respect and trust is what appreciation is all about.

An Attitude of Gratitude

Appreciating the teens in your charge means that you know and acknowledge their worth, that you understand the importance of who they are as individuals.

Appreciation is all about gratitude. Think about how grateful you are to have them in your life. How sad would you be if they were gone? If you can find ways to show how much you value these goofy, yet fun and interesting creatures, you will be on your way to fully expressing your appreciation to the teens you are so lucky to have in your life.

Consider for a moment all the people who do not have the opportunity that you've been given to work with them. Teenagers, as frustrating as they can be sometimes, are a gift from God. They are like the Christmas gift you get from Great Aunt Nell; the one you really aren't quite sure what to do with, but appreciate nonetheless.

Mind Your Manners

We have all been taught, at one time or another, to say please and thank you. We were trained to be courteous. Some of us remember those lessons from our youth and some of us have gotten too busy and distracted to bother. It's time to reinstate the simple courtesies. When you ask your teens for help, say please. After helping, say thank you.

Simple? Yes. Important? Absolutely. The simple act of saying please and thank you shows your teens that you appreciate what they do. Take it a step further by making a batch of their favorite cookies or giving them a gift card when they go out of their way to help.

Just as you work to show your teens how much you appreciate them being a part of your life, teach them the importance of appreciating all they have in theirs. Appreciation is a reciprocal kind of thing. Appreciating others allows us to feel more appreciated.

The teenage years are naturally a time when it's difficult to be grateful. Teens are trying to establish their independence. They are desperate to express their individuality. It's normal and it's healthy. It's a natural rung on the ladder toward independent adulthood. It takes a little more time and a little more maturity before they realize how much they have to be grateful for.

Helping teens to regain their own sense of gratitude will go a long way in showing them that they, themselves, are appreciated. They will respect the lessons you're trying to teach, will appreciate you for your effort, and will, in turn, understand that what you do stems from the appreciation you have for them.

Gratitude Journal

It's a simple technique that has been around for a while because it's so effective. Teach your teens to use a gratitude journal. Sure, they might think it's a silly idea at first. But, they will begin to see the value of noticing the small things around them and it's something you can even do with them.

Set aside regular times to have your teens write in their journals when you first begin the practice. If necessary, provide the notebooks and the pencils and fun pens. When you're finished with the activity, lock the notebooks up somewhere in the house so they'll know that no prying eyes can see what they have written.

Start by giving them a prompt, such as: "Today I'm grateful for these things:" Set a time limit of 15 or 20 minutes and ask them simply to write. They should not be concerned with spelling or grammar. Remind them that this is for their eyes only. It won't be evaluated by their overly picky English teacher. Encourage them to write non-stop. Anything and everything for which they feel gratitude should be included.

After a few sessions with the gratitude journal,

you'll start to see some amazing things. They'll begin to request time to write in their journals. They'll begin to ask if they can carry their journals with them so they can write whenever they want to. And most excitingly, you'll begin to hear a new sense of gratitude in their voices and in their casual conversations. They will begin to notice more and more things to be grateful for. And they will be grateful to you for increasing their own appreciation.

Mirror, Mirror

Mirror, mirror on the wall, who's the most appreciative one of all? Children, teens included, mirror what they see around them. Showing teens that you appreciate them will teach them how to appreciate others. When teenagers see you being appreciative of them, and others, they will begin to see how much better life can be when we all feel that we have the support and appreciation of others.

Ways to Teach Being Grateful

- Let them see how you are grateful, even for small things.
- Let them see and hear you say thank you.

- Talk to them about your appreciation – especially of them.
- Don't complain.
- Model the gratitude journal and share your entries.
- Let them see that you appreciate the beauty of nature and other things that many people take for granted.

No Fault Zone

Of course, your teens have faults, as do we all. But dwelling on those faults only proves to our teens that we don't appreciate them so much after all. If you want to cultivate appreciation in your teens, you must model respect. We teach by example, so be sure that you're not just telling them what to do, but also doing what you say.

Try not to be judgmental. Judgments are dishonoring. Appreciation is honoring. Judgments close teenagers down. When they feel they are being judged, they will come back at you defensively. And who can blame them? Remember Mark Twain? We all like compliments much more than we do criticisms. Treating your teens with respect and dignity will make them feel loved and valued.

It's also important not to judge or criticize when your teens share their lives. Negative judgments are really the opposite of appreciation. It's saying that we disapprove. Appreciation, on the other hand, displays interest. When we are appreciative, we are curious. We want to know more about this person we appreciate. Of course, you don't want to appear nosey. Teens most definitely will not appreciate that. But, showing that you genuinely care for your teens as individuals, that you're interested in a non-judgmental, non-critical way in their friends, interests, hopes and dreams, says that you appreciate them for who they are.

Appreciation in Action - Celebrate their Individuality

Don't let the teens you are around get lost in the busyness of life. Set aside time to talk to your teens individually or in very small groups. You'll get to know who they are, what their interests are and what goals they have for the future.

You can create opportunities to spend individual time with your teens. If you need to run to the store, take a couple of your teens with you while the rest are left to continue on with the project at hand. Just be sure to spread your individual time equally throughout the entire group.

Show Your Trust

Show your teens that you trust them by letting them help in ways that are needed. Let them know you believe they are dependable and that you can rely on them. Rather than doing it yourself, after all, you are busy too and they see this, let them make the needed run to the store. Toss them the keys to the van. Send a couple of them together. They will know that you are trusting them to fulfill a needed demand. Be sure to thank them when they return.

If you have a job to do in the kitchen, select three teens who've displayed amazing kitchen talents - even if it's that they seem to do a good job on clean up and don't mind. Tell them how much you appreciate those talents and ask the three to go on cleanup duty. Allowing them to work together and chatting without your interference, will give them time to engage in teen talk. They will appreciate your trust and that you have given them this time. They'll see it as a sign of your appreciation.

Let them Be

Give your teens a chance to express themselves creatively. Try not to cringe when they show up to a meeting in purple hair. The teen years are years of exploration. The ripped jeans, the funky tee-shirts and pierced eyebrows, the crazy hairdo's and even the gigantic holes in their ears are all a relatively benign part of their figuring out who they are.

If you can build a trusting, respectful relationship by appreciating who they are and how they choose to express themselves, they'll be more likely to return that appreciation and respect. They will probably even be willing to tone down those looks if and when you think it's important. If you're going out into the business world, for example, setting a dress code is totally acceptable. Letting them dress how they want to 90% of the time will give you license to set some standards occasionally. Just explain why. Talk about how appearances count in certain situations. If you've set the stage with appreciation and respect, they will listen and cooperate.

Engage Them

Talk to your teens. Talk about what movies they

have seen, the current video game that is all the rage, school, current events, etc. Teens love to talk. Engaging them to talk about what matters to them is expressing interest in who they are. The more you talk, the more comfortable they'll become and the more they will be willing to share. They will see that you appreciate their attitudes and opinions. They'll see that you are truly interested in hearing what they have to say. Remember, again, not to be judgmental, no matter how crazy and radical you might think their views are. Don't argue or insist that they see your point of view, however right you might be.

Be open and willing to discuss controversial topics. Teens love to debate. And remember while they are arguing, they are still trying to determine what they really think about these issues, even if they say and act as if they have it all figured out. Most of them know they really don't know. If you can offer up the facts, if you can help them explore both sides of whatever topic is on the table, they'll learn to appreciate you for your calm, unbiased reason and they'll see that you appreciate their opinions as well.

The more you talk with them, the more likely they will be to come to you when they have an important issue they need help with. They will have learned that you appreciate and respect who they are and that you will lend a listening ear, and perhaps even be able to help.

Show them How Much You Care

Some teens are hard to love. Usually those are the teens that need your love the most. They will act out because the teenage years can be so difficult for so many of them. They will be disrespectful. They will drive you nuts. Not always. But sometimes.

And when they do, you need to take a deep breath and show them how much you care. Rather than over-reacting and taking their missteps personally, relax and realize that they are simply being teens, an awkward and uncertain animal at best. Rather than getting angry, try really hard to shrug your shoulders and say, "It's okay." Give them a hug. Tell them that you understand.

Appreciate the chance to have a learning moment. Not by lecturing, but by relaxing and reacting in a way that shows how much you care.

A Chance to Change a Life

The importance of showing and receiving appreciation is nothing new. Born in 1878, Margaret Cousins, an Irish-Indian educator, said, "Appreciation can make a day, even change a life. Your willingness to put it into words is all that is necessary."

Those of us who work with teens know how troubling their lives can be. We've seen how some of them must struggle. We've seen them make questionable choices. But we've also seen their resilience. We've witnessed first-hand the strength some teens display as they work to overcome whatever obstacles their lives have placed before them.

These are the teens that need us the most. These are the teens who need to be recognized and appreciated for not only what they do, but for who they are. Not only do they need this type of acknowledgement, they deserve it.

As you work to find new and engaging ways to appreciate your teens, don't forget that sincerity is the quickest path to showing your appreciation. Simply recognizing your teens can work wonders.

Saying, "Hello! How are you today?" and then waiting for an answer tells your teens that you care. It's not an obligatory greeting you're throwing out. It's a warm and genuine welcome. It's an invitation to your teen. You want to hear about his day, about his life, about him.

Finally, be sure to appreciate your role, the one you get to play in the lives of your teens. The most wonderful part of all this is that we are the lucky ones. We are the ones who get to appreciate these teens and see our appreciation of them shining back through their eyes onto us.

Chapter 2 Questions for Reflection/Discussion

1. You come into the group room and your teens are talking about one of their teachers at school. They are complaining and name calling, saying he is a terrible teacher and doesn't care about his students at all. They say he doesn't know what he's doing and that they are going to stop listening and stop doing their work. After all, they argue, they're not learning anything anyway. How might you handle this?

2. Brainstorm ways in which you can show your appreciation, with your words and your actions, for your teens. What ways can you show appreciation in your words and actions for both the group as a whole and for each as individuals?

3. A couple of your teens have hooked up with a group at school that is very gothic. They wear dark, gothic clothing and accessories. They seem to be more and more enamored with this "goth," occult-like new group of friends. You worry where this might be

leading. What could you say or do to connect with these teens?

4. You have started a campaign to show your teens how much you appreciate them. You've vocalized your appreciation and are spending more time talking with them about what matters most to them. You believe you are creating a stronger bond with the entire group and are pleased with your relationship. You then hear a group of your teens talking about your new efforts, saying that they don't believe you are sincere. They seem to think you are playing a game of sorts, being nice so that you can get them to work harder for the program. How might you respond?

Chapter 3: Teenagers Need Honest Affection

When children are small, they want nothing more than loving attention from the adults in their world: a hand to hold or a lap to sit on. Other than wiping noses, primary school teachers spend more time handing out hugs than they have energy for. However, as they grow and develop, teenagers are much harder to read. That's because, when it comes to affection, they aren't really sure what they do or do not want.

That's okay. They needn't decide. As loving, caring adults, we know that, although, they may say they don't want or need our affection, they do. And we are here to provide it.

Dr. Laurence Steinberg, author and leading authority on adolescence, poignantly reminds us that, "[A child] will not be harmed by being told every single day that you love him. Your child will not be hurt by being showered with physical affection, with care and with praise when it's heartfelt and well deserved. Don't hold back your affection or act aloof because you think your child will become spoiled by all the attention." It's a perfect reminder that love never hurt anyone.

A Distancing Act

As our teens begin to distance themselves in a search for and show of independence, the touchy-feely stuff becomes more than just uninvited. It becomes an annoyance. They pull away with a grimace. They respond with a verbal "Yuck," a nonverbal cold shoulder or even one of each. One mom shared that putting her arms around her teen is like trying to hug a porcupine.

That does not mean, however, that we shouldn't try. Do not take any rejection you may receive personally. Teens absolutely want to be loved. They want us to reach out to them. They want us to remind them that they are lovable and that they are loved. They want that show of attention and affection, even as they are strong-arming away our attempts.

And honestly, although they'd say they don't, they truly appreciate all your efforts in showing them sincere and honest affection. So rather than accepting their indifference, keep trying. Keep telling them how much you care. It means so much. It tells them that they are worth your love, which is truly the most important thing in their lives.

The Journey Begins

As children begin to grow and search for that sense of independence, many begin to push aside the things they now see as childish. Some view the things they liked to do when they were younger as now way too immature to enjoy as a teen. They want to be more grown up. Giving and accepting affection is sometimes a part of what they now see as childish. "I'm not a baby anymore," they tell the world. They desperately want to redefine themselves as young adults, but they struggle to find ways to do so.

As a result, teens can become unresponsive. You show your affection and they show you a scowl. You offer up a hug and they shirk at your attempts. This certainly does not mean that your teens do not want and, more importantly, do not need your affection. You must continue to offer it. You must continue to find ways to express how much you care. Through both physical and verbal affection, your teens will begin to understand that they can count on you.

Truthfully, many of our teens need more affection than they will admit they want and they often need more affection than they, in reality, get. Some of this lack is, of course, because they are withdrawing from those ready to bestow that affection. Some of this lack is a natural part of mothers and fathers learning how to continue to show affection to their children of the opposite gender. And some of this lack is due to parents answering the calls, or rather the grunts and groans of their teens, and believing that their children no longer want or need to be shown affection.

But the absolute truth is that these growing and maturing beings continue to have a very real need for affection. Don't we all?

How to Show You Care

If you've worked with younger children, you know how much easier it comes when building a relationship with them. All you have to do is sit them in a circle, hold hands and tell a fun story. You are their hero for life.

Teens, as we know, are far more difficult to convince. "Sure," they think, "This guy/gal says he/she cares about me, but why should I believe that? And even more, why would I accept any affection from him/her? After all, I'm thirteen/sixteen/eighteen years old! No huggy-bear/kissy-face for me. I am an adult!"

Never forget, though, that these teens need us and they need our honest affection. Be persistent. Showing your non-threatening, but sincerely genuine affection works. It impacts the lives of teenagers. And when it does, you'll reap truly grand rewards. You'll be their hero for life.

Those Three Little Words

It's a little tricky to say "I love you" when you work with other people's teens. The boundaries of both verbal and physical affection are different than when you are dealing with younger children or children of your own. I believe, however, that it's okay to tell your teens that you love them. Say it to the group. Say it lightly. You can even say it with humor. But say it.

And say it often. "I love you guys." Simple, non-threatening and very effective. "You goof-balls are the best. I love each and every one of you."

Act as Though You Like Them (Because You Do)

Teens are smart. You can give them all the hugs and metaphorical kisses you'd like, but if you don't like who they are as individuals, they'll know it. So, be sure to act as though you like them. In fact, you do like them, so be sure they realize it. They will interpret that genuine fondness as honest affection, because it is. Spending time with them, sharing their interests, really talking to them and being interested in what they have to say are all ways to show your honest affection. They'll feel it, they'll believe it and they'll respond to it.

Remain Rock Solid

Reaffirm that you are there for them. Many teens today live in dysfunctional homes. Some have literally been abandoned and live without their parents. Others live without much affection at all, which is why it is so important that you build an affectionate relationship with each and every one of them. Only then will they trust that you will continue to be there for them. They will begin to rely on you, and it's up to you not to let them down. Even when they are irritating and irksome, your honest, sincere affection must remain as solid ground beneath their feet. They must know that they can count on you to be there. You will not abandon them.

Hug and Run

Similar to a hit and run, only much warmer and fuzzier, is the hug and run. A little nudge, a ruffle of the hair, a couple of quick (and gentle) taps on the cheek or chin all say, "I care about you." And because you do it fast and furious and then are gone, you haven't made a big messy ordeal of the affection. Your teens will appreciate the subtlety. In fact, don't even look back as you go. Your teens may be making faces but, trust me, they understand what you're up to and they appreciate it. Even if you hear them grimacing aloud, be persistent. You love them. Period. End of story. Nothing to be ashamed of and you're not to be deterred. They'll get it. And whether they show you or not, they will love you back.

The Touchy-Feely Stuff

Just as it is when you tell other people's teens that you love them, it can be equally awkward or even more so to give them any type of physical affection. It is, however, equally important. They may get too uncomfortable and start to squirm if you go in for a bear hug, but you can certainly give them a pat on the back. You can give them a double high five. You can give them a little head rub or simply grab their shoulders and look them in the eye as you say, "Great job." The demonstrations of your affection don't have to be huge or even long-lasting. But they need to be honest and sincere.

Go slowly when you see that any of the teens in your charge are overly uncomfortable with your attempts at physical affection. They may be wounded by past experiences. Expressing your honest affection through what you say can help teens begin to open up to accepting your affection in a more physical way. A loving word and a sincere smile can help them begin to heal. And perhaps you'll find that any type of physical displays simply doesn't work. That's okay. But never give up on finding ways to show how much you sincerely and genuinely care.

Teenage boys can be especially difficult to get through to, and yet it is the boys in your charge who may need your affection the most. They are growing up and trying to be manly. Just proceed with conscientious awareness. Girls tend to be easier. They aren't threatened by your affection and are used to the touchy-feely girl stuff. They are used to sharing their emotions and their affections with their friends.

Just understand how important it is to help these young people learn to accept your honest affection. Loving affection is a primal need for all.

Detached and Alone

Although fairly uncommon, understand that some children and teens suffer from attachment issues. When the deep and necessary connection between a child and his parents is not established for whatever reason, the child's ability to develop relationships is profoundly harmed. Children suffering from an attachment disorder are unable to build loving, meaningful relationships because they cannot connect with others. They have no trust in relationships. They are afraid of becoming close for a fear of being abandoned. They have no sense of security.

Teens who have been repeatedly abandoned or neglected learn that they cannot depend on a relationship with others. They see the world as a very dangerous, frightful place. Getting through to a teen who has an attachment disorder can be frustrating. It can take a lot of time and effort to slowly build a caring relationship that the teen can eventually begin to trust. However, it is worth the effort. Without the skills to create loving relationships, these kids can be lost forever; never to trust or establish a bond with another human being. With a lot of love and plenty of patience, though, the damage this child has suffered can be repaired. And what a wonderful gift you are giving as you literally restore his or her faith in mankind.

A Celebration of the Affectionate Kind

Showing sincere and honest affection is also vital in helping your teens develop that all-important sense of self-worth. Celebrating who your teens are, paying attention to them as individuals and showing them how much you care helps them to grow and develop into caring people themselves. Consistently sending an affectionate message, whether it's through your words, a smile, a squeeze of the shoulders or sharing a candy bar you just scored from the vending machine in the hallway, will have your teens seeing your love and respect of them as real.

Another way to show your honest affection and celebrate who your teens are is by remembering and celebrating important moments in their lives. Make note of and celebrate their birthdays. Always, always, wish your teens a happy birthday. It may not seem like a big deal to you, but it is to them, even if they say it isn't. Consider having a seasonal birthday party and doing it up right. Schedule a birthday party once a quarter and include the honorees whose birthdays land within those dates. You might even start a tradition of having each birthday teen share something about his or her life. You might encourage them to create a poster collage displaying what's important to them. Musical students might write a song to perform and/or gifted writers could write a poem. Anything that says "You are special and today we recognize you" is a wonderful way to express the honest affection you have for each and every one of your teens.

Asking Nothing in Return

Showing your teens how much you care must be an unconditional commitment. When they are troublesome, which they most certainly will be, you cannot withhold your affection. Sure, you're going to get frustrated. You may even get downright mad. And that's okay. They probably deserve it. But try not to explode into some sort of critical rant that could do damage to the teen and to your relationship.

That does not mean that you cannot be honest about your anger. Just try to show your anger calmly. It is absolutely essential that kids know they are loved. Even though they messed up big time, even though you're obviously quite angry, they must know that you still love and respect them. You love them for who they are, not for what they do. You love them because they are a beautiful, perfect creation of God, not because they swept the group room floor.

A truly genuine and unconditional affection is one that is given freely in the face of failure. In fact, it may be in the face of failure when your teens need your affection the most. We all get frustrated with ourselves. We all have those days when it seems that no one really cares, when it seems as though we're going it alone. Teens do too. It is on these less-than-good days that they need us the most. Our teens will know our feelings are genuine if we can offer up that honest affection on the really bad days. They will know that the relationship we've worked to build with them is real and lasting. And, perhaps most importantly, they will know that they are okay. They will know that they are worthy, even in their times of failure. They will also know that it's worth shaking off the failure and trying again.

Your teens will learn they are fundamentally good and deserving individuals when they are given unconditional love and honest affection. When they are offered conditional love, love which is given in the good times and withheld in the bad, teens learn that they are not fundamentally acceptable. They begin to believe they are only deserving of love when they are good, which none of us are all the time. Some of the teens with whom we work with may have been conditioned to believe they are only worthy when they win. This type of harmful reinforcement creates anxiety and fear. It may teach the teen to win at all costs, but those wins quickly lose their sparkle.

As you continue to show your affection for your

teens, know that you are helping them to develop confidence and self-esteem. As you model affection, you show them that affection is a good and positive thing. It's not something of which to be embarrassed or ashamed about. It's a loving gesture that we all need. You are also setting them up to build affectionate relationships in their future, which is so important for all of us.

A Final Bid for Affection

Our teens need so much from us. They need us to be there, to be nurturing and warm, to be gentle and kind and caring and strong. They need us to define boundaries for their behavior. They need us to guide them along as they struggle on the path to adulthood. They need us to cheer them on and let them know they are okay - that they are traveling the right road and making good time.

Truly one of the most important gifts we can give these teens is our honest, sincere affection. Our teens will understand in the moments when we fail to give them what they need at the appropriate time, if we consistently show our affection. They will see these failures of ours as simply missteps, not as an overall lack of caring. We aren't perfect. They aren't perfect. When a relationship is built on absolute sincere affection, none of that matters. Perfection is never the goal. The real goal is a growing, learning and loving connection.

As you shower your teens with affection, know that you are helping them develop into confident, secure adults who will be able to build strong and lasting relationships with others. When our teens feel our love, all - or at least most - things become right with the world.

Understand that you shouldn't fear setting limits for your teens. You not only can, but you certainly should continue to define boundaries for their behavior. As you do so, however, continue to show your affection. The teens in your charge must always know that any discipline or consequences for their behavior in no way reflects any diminished affection you feel for them. So, even as you're doling out the reprimands, make sure they know you love them.

You will be rewarded ten-fold for your efforts. Your teens will respond with honest affection of their own and it will be directed toward you.

Chapter 3 Questions for Reflection/Discussion

1. One of the teens in your charge continues to isolate himself from you and from the group. None of your attempts at showing him honest affection have been successful. He is withdrawn and often borders on being recalcitrant. How can you bring him into the group more actively?

2. Several of your more frustrating teens have begun a mini-rebellion of sorts. They are rabble-rousing, difficult and unresponsive at your attempts of showing any type of affection. When you get to the bottom of the trouble, you find that the main instigator is a teen who was abandoned as a very young child and, because of his habit of causing trouble, has been passed around through several foster homes. What might you do to help this teen?

3. A mother comes to you and expresses extreme displeasure at your small and non-intrusive shows of affection toward her child. How might you handle this?

4. Although your attempts to show your group honest affection have been sincere and, in your eyes, completely fair and impartial, a few teens approach you saying you are playing favorites. It is obvious, in their eyes, that you have what they call "pets." How you might respond?

Chapter 4: Teenagers Need Unconditional Acceptance

Accepting our teens unconditionally is the greatest, most loving and nurturing gift we can give. When we accept our teens exactly as they are - in this exact place and at this exact time - we allow them to see how valuable they truly are - in our eyes and in the eyes of God.

Our unconditional acceptance allows teens, who are insecure by nature, to understand that their strengths and their weaknesses, their brilliance and their silliness, their successes and their failures are all interwoven to create the amazingly unique individuals they are.

We also show them that giving them our acceptance unconditionally isn't about waving a white flag. It isn't about giving them permission to give up and no longer work to do and to be better. Instead, it's an approving nod of who they are, who we all are, in the present moment. It's a loving salute that can heal the deepest wound and renew the most troubled soul.

Understand that you are not going to be perfect at this. You are not going to be able to love unconditionally all the time. You may get tired. You may get distracted. You may even get angry. But these emotional states need not deter you from accepting unconditionally. Just as your teens will undoubtedly have bad days, you, too, may have a bad day. If you can be honest with yourself and with your teens, a bad day will not be the end of the strong bond that unconditional acceptance builds. As long as you show up, as long as you are present and attentive and persistent, your teens will feel your love.

Teenage Angst

We all know how difficult it is to be a teenager. After all, we used to be teens, however long ago. A huge part of the difficulty that teens face comes from anxiety, what we call teenage "angst." Teenagers face an uncertain future and their anxiety is real. Who wouldn't be anxious staring out into that vast unknown?

The array of concerns that teens endure spread out before them in the form of questions: Who will I be? Will I be a success? Will someone love me? Will I find a job and have a family and live the life I want to live?

And as if all the uncertainty is not enough, in the midst of the questions comes peer pressure. As these young people try to figure out who they really are, they look to their friends for clues. Oftentimes they find themselves being someone they are not. They do things they might not otherwise do. They worry about being in the popular crowd. They worry about what Suzy told Johnny who told Emily what Erica said.

These fears and worries are not to be dismissed. The teen years are a moratorium of sorts. They are a time for teens to begin to understand who they will become. The biggest step towards helping a teen through these turbulent years is making sure they know that they are loved. They must know they are accepted. Fully. Totally. Unconditionally.

Providing such unconditional acceptance is not always the easiest of tasks. Because of the turmoil they feel, which, remember is quite real, a teen's attitude and behavior can be less than pleasant. But if we are to have a real effect in their lives, we must relax and enjoy the ride. As we work to teach and mold and guide our teens, we must love and accept them unconditionally, exactly as they are.

The Value of a Teenager

So many of today's teenagers have low self-esteem. Some, in fact, have no self-esteem at all. Because of their adolescent insecurities, teens tend to underestimate their own value, not realizing they have much more to contribute than they might imagine. The reasons for this are as varied as the teens are themselves. Much of it comes from a lack of parenting or appropriate role-models. Much of it comes from the belief that they do not live up to either real or imagined expectations. Sometimes the expectations are those they place upon themselves. Other times it's the expectations that we, either knowingly or unknowingly, place on them. When they feel they are less than expected, they experience a sense of shame, which quickly translates into low self-esteem.

As teenagers try to find themselves, they are desperately trying to fit in and to make sense of a world that doesn't always make sense. Very often, as adults, we forget what it was like to be a teenager. We forget that a teen's world is filled with confusion and apprehension.

Low self-esteem makes young people angry and/or anxious. It makes them fear challenges and opportunities, leaving them to begin a downward spiral, feeling worse and worse about themselves. Sadly, when this happens, they are left to seek out people and experiences that will make them feel better. These are often people and experiences that are less than good for them.

To teach teens how to feel good about who they are, we need to let them know that what they think or say or feel or do is okay. That doesn't mean that the behavior should continue if it is inappropriate. It means that we must help them understand that they are not the first, nor will they be the last, to feel this way. It means we need to let them know that we are all doing the best we can at the time. We might have done better but we didn't. Next time we will. We all make mistakes. We are all human beings.

Building Blocks to Self-Esteem

Helping teens develop stronger self-esteem is a matter of treating them as though they are valuable. When you smile or offer a kind word, when you give a high-five for a job well done or even when you enforce a rule with discipline, you show your teens that you care -that they are worth your time. When the teens in your charge know you care, when they see that you're willing to take time to pay attention, they begin to believe that they have value.

Offer Up Plenty of Praise

It's so easy to tell kids what they are doing wrong. We need to be generous in telling them what they are doing right to help them find a sense of their own worth. "Catch them being good," parents of toddlers are told. The lesson is equally valid for those who work with teens.

Encouraging the pursuits of teens, no matter what those pursuits may be, is a sure way to help them grow in their own self-acceptance. Be a cheerleader as you continue to get to know your teens. If a teen wants to become a movie star, encourage him to join the local drama team. It's important not to dismiss the dreams and goals of teenagers, even if you think they are silly or out of reach. Your smiling affirmations and the confidence you display in them will help them gain the confidence they need to find within themselves. Sure, you may think that movie stardom is out of reach, and perhaps it is, but they'll figure that out themselves, if and when it's time.

When a child is truly trying, whether he is two or twelve or seventeen, his efforts should be acknowledged. When we show that we are sincerely proud of them, our teens can begin to feel proud of themselves. Applauding the effort is also an important way to teach our teens that we're not only proud of what they've done. We are proud who they are.

Criticize Constructively

Teens are more intuitive than you might think, and they need to be told the truth. If they have made a poor choice, they most likely already know it. If you're insincerely positive or remain quiet when criticism needs to be made, they will see you as disingenuous, which is one of the quickest way to lose their respect.

However, when you need to provide criticism or reprimands, it's important to do so in a constructive manner. Their feelings will be hurt if you are hurtful or demeaning, even if you don't intend to be, which can create a lasting wound that will be difficult to heal. The teen years are emotional; their hormones are raging. So rather than saying, "How could you have done that?" with that being whatever they've done wrong, you might instead say, "You missed the boat on that one; you'll get it right next time."

Ask their Opinion

Teens have many opinions. Ask any one of them their view on anything and you'll get plenty of responses. Let them air their opinions on what matters to them. And if you can include them in a decision-making process when it affects them, and even when it doesn't directly affect them, they will see that you value their input. For example, let them help decide where the next outing will be. Or what specifics should be included in the next event. Or even what color the youth room should be painted and how it should be furnished. When you respect their opinions, which is really the same as respecting their voice, you show that you trust and respect them for the individuals they are. They'll see your trust and respect as acceptance and a vote of confidence, which will help them develop confidence in themselves.

Cheer Them On

Everyone is really good at something and the teens in your charge are no different. Whatever passion your teen has is what he or she should be encouraged to do. Even if you think that sketching video game avatars is a waste of time, he or she should be encouraged, especially if the teen is really good at it. After all, drawing is an amazing talent. Support that talent. In doing so, you'll be accepting your teen's interests and helping him build confidence and strong self-esteem.

As you encourage their talents, help the teens with whom you work to see that striving to do their best is what's most important. They don't have to be perfect. None of us are.

You might even consider holding a talent program to showcase the talents your teens have. They'll get to show off their work to adults, and although they would deny this to the death, they love to show off.

They will bask in the glory of applause and come away feeling better about who they are and their abilities. They'll learn that they have something of value to contribute, an understanding essential to becoming self-accepting, responsible and contributing members of society.

Let Them Dream

Teens are very idealistic. As adults, we might think that teens are downright naïve. "We should all live on an island, grow our own food and live in peace." Do not laugh when your teens express their idealism. Remember, we were all young once and most of us had those definitive, "if only" answers as to how to change the world. Rather than being cynical, rather than demanding they recognize the realities of this harsh world in which we live, let them dream. Remember that the real answer to making this harsh world in which we live a better place lies with the dreaming youth of today.

A Case for Compassion

Compassion is about seeing another person's wounds and wanting to help. And believe me when I tell you that many of today's teens are wounded.

They need our help.

Being compassionate can require a little practice, especially if you are dealing with an unruly teenager or two. When you have compassion, however, it is much easier to be the loving and understanding mentor you need to be. Suddenly you understand what these goofy teens are going through. Suddenly it's a little easier to forgive their missteps. Suddenly you are walking through life with them as you gain their trust.

Celebrate the Individual

Commit to being compassionate in each and every encounter with your teens. If you notice irritation creeping in, stop. Take a breath and find something to appreciate about whoever has sparked that irritation. Be concrete and specific. Perhaps you appreciate this teenager's smile. Perhaps you appreciate another's sense of humor.

If you can approach each and every day with compassion for yourself and all those you encounter, including the teens in your charge, you'll begin to notice a change not only in your teens but also in yourself. With compassion comes respect, which quickly translates into acceptance.

Speak Softly

Teens are sensitive. They may act as though they are tough and indestructible, but they aren't. Many are frightened little children in grown-up bodies. Remember to treat your teens gently.

Treat them lovingly.

It's important to try to avoid sarcasm, which is sometimes difficult because it's the language in which most teens speak. Of course, you must keep your sense of humor and teens love wit, but don't let your responses disintegrate into hurtful sarcasm, which can be demeaning. You take a chance of losing the teens you work with forever if they become hurt or discouraged.

And, of course, you may have to call your teenagers out for their poor behavior and/or bad choices. But do so gently. Do not say, "You should be ashamed of yourself." You can tell them what to do and how to do it, but you should never ask them to take on shame. They have plenty of that internally or from others without placing more on them.

Community Service

A truly great way to show your teens that they have, and deserve to have, your unconditional acceptance is by organizing community service projects.

Planning community service outings is an effective way to get teens to see how much value they have to add to the world. Giving teens a chance to help others may be the SINGLE BEST way to show that you appreciate them and to let them appreciate themselves.

There are so many teenagers who are insecure; they might never consider that they can fulfill an expectation for improving another person's life. Volunteer work, for which expectations aren't quite so demanding, can let them see that they are able to rise to whatever challenges and meet whatever expectations the project demands. They will gain a sense of pride and independence that will allow them to begin to accept themselves.

Working together to help the community is also one of the best ways to get kids to recognize that they are a valuable part of that community. They begin to understand what others need and to gain an appreciation for what they, themselves, have. They will understand how helping others makes them feel good about themselves. And they will gain the respect and attention of those they help, which will confirm that they are worth respecting. When teens experience sincere gratitude for having served, they will glow with pride, which translates into self-acceptance and self-esteem.

Allow Yourself a Break

Take a break when you need to. It's hard to work with kids. They have so much energy and enthusiasm. They are silly. They are moody. They are hard to keep up with. They are always something and many are always needy. When you find that your nerves are becoming shot, do yourself and them a favor and take a break. Ask any middle or high school teacher. You will be far better for yourself and for your teens if you step back occasionally. You cannot do what you need to do, such as giving them what they need emotionally, if you're feeling depleted. It's only when your own cup is full that you can help to fill the cup of others.

Unconditional Love

Unconditional acceptance is unconditional love, and both are about letting teens understand that they are loved, that they are accepted, that they have value NO MATTER WHAT. It's not about loving a behavior or an attitude. It's about loving who they are at their very core. And who they are is the unique individual that God created them to be. They will be on their way to fulfilling the uniquely individual purpose God has set for them with your unconditional acceptance.

When you love unconditionally, you express a sincere appreciation for each of your teen's individuality. You share in their sorrows and celebrate their joys, focusing on the inherent singularity of each as an individual. You allow them to be who they truly are, not someone trying to make you happy, but a very special and unique person. In this way, teenagers learn to accept themselves. They learn who they are and who they are meant to be.

Unconditional acceptance is a love that remains firm through the hardest of times. It's not based on certain conditions or on particular requirements. Those who grow up being accepted unconditionally develop an emotional strength which carries them throughout life. They develop an inner strength and self-acceptance that prepares them to blossom into the strong and loving person they are meant to be. It is a beautiful thing that you, as a mentor and teacher and guide, can be the beginning of an amazing transformation in the teens you love.

Chapter 4 Questions for Reflection/Discussion

1. A teen comes to you and, in confidence, tells you that he has decided to quit school. He pleads with you not to tell his parents and says that you are the only adult who accepts him for who he is. He goes on to explain that who he is, is not someone who is going to finish high school. What might you do to connect and encourage him to make a good life decision?

2. Brainstorm as many reasons as you can as to why teens today have such low self-esteem. Consider as many complicating issues as you can: home and family, school, friends, community, world, etc. What are the biggest reasons based on your observations?

3. You enter the youth room to find two girls engaged in a physical battle. With some difficulty and no help from their peers, you get the two separated. You have always been especially close to one of the girls; she has been respectful and helpful. The other

girl has been reserved, sulky and disengaged. What would you say to each girl, both separately and together? What would you say to the group? What other consequences might you impart or measures might you take?

4. To your dismay, you realize that a group of your teens have been involved in an exceptionally hurtful episode of cyber-bullying toward an unpopular teen at their school. How might you handle the situation? What would you say and do to facilitate accountability and a positive outcome?

Chapter 5: Teenagers Need Consistent Accountability

The 2004 movie Hotel Rwanda explored the real-life drama of Rwanda as it suffered from political corruption and genocide. The film showed hotel manager Paul Rusesabagina rescue more than a thousand refugees by offering them shelter in his besieged hotel. As the country's political situation grew increasingly more dangerous, the hotel manager threatened his own personal security to keep his family and fellow Rwandans safe. In so doing, he became a beacon of hope and strength and the savior of thousands who would have otherwise been killed.

It's a story of accountability. Paul Rusesabagina accepted the consequences of his own behavior. Carrying truth and faith as his sword, he risked everything to do what he knew in his heart to be right.

This kind of accountability does not always come naturally. Taking responsibility for one's actions can be difficult. It can be especially difficult for young people. We as pastors, parents, teachers and mentors must help the teenagers we serve by lovingly, yet firmly, guiding them along as they learn to become honest, reliable, accountable adults.

Understanding a Teen's Reality

Research shows that the brains of adolescents do not fully develop until they reach their early 20's. Teenagers do not yet have a mature sense of right and wrong, nor do they have a mature sense of accountability. With our help, however, they can grow to become accountable, successful adults.

Part of the struggle that teens have with accountability comes from the fact that many are living lives much different than we did when we were teens ourselves. Because life for many teens is filled with chaos, they struggle to respond appropriately to the difficulties that surround them. Rather than responding in logical, mature ways, they respond emotionally. When teens see dysfunction in their families, in their schools and in society at large, they tend to display behaviors that are chaotic and dysfunctional.

It is up to the caring adults in their lives to guide them toward a calmer, more functional way to respond to life's challenges. We must teach them to take responsibility for their own actions, which is what accountability is all about. We must help them learn to set boundaries and to take responsibility for their own behavior.

Creating a Climate of Accountability

The first step in helping teenagers understand and then develop a sense of responsibility is to create an environment of accountability. When teens recognize that we, as the adults in their world, take accountability for our actions, they begin to accept accountability as an appropriate behavior. If we take responsibility for our own actions and expect them to do the same, we create a culture of accountability. When teenagers know that we are all in this together, they are more likely to not only accept, but to become engaged with, the importance of being responsible.

Accountability Gone Wrong

Although you may suspect the contrary, teenagers pay attention. They see that taking responsibility for one's actions is not what many people do. Our athletes, our celebrities and our affluent society does not always hold these people accountable. The news is filled with stories of the rich and famous being less than accountable. As adults, we shake our heads and wonder what has happened to the world.

Teenagers, however, are watching, listening and learning. They see these news bytes as reflections of reality. After all, their favorite sports figures and movie stars are getting away with poor choices. So what's a little irresponsibility going to hurt? Allowing this premise to go unchallenged is, in effect, raising ethically challenged teens who go on to become ethically challenged adults. We do the teens we care about a disservice if we don't challenge the lack of accountability we see around us.

Helping teens grow and develop within a climate of accountability is about helping them understand the standards by which they choose to live. It's about helping them find their moral compass and learning how not to compromise their beliefs. It's about guiding them to make good choices and own up to their behavior when they don't make the best decisions.

Walk the Talk

It is of the utmost importance that teens see the adults in their world taking responsibility. There should be none of this "Do as I say, not as I do" type of methodology when you're working with teenagers. When we model respect, truth and honesty, when we are accountable for our own actions, young people see that they can trust us. They begin to listen to what we have to say. If they see that we have a sincere desire to positively impact their lives and to keep them safe, they develop confidence in our words. When they see us taking responsibility for our own behavior, they learn that taking accountability is a part of having integrity.

One thing we can do to create an environment of accountability is to always be present in their lives. Paying attention to what our teenagers are doing is a means of showing our presence. It shows that we care about them and the choices they make. It doesn't mean they are forever under our thumb. It does mean that we check in. We communicate. And when we model making good choices based on our care for one another and for the world in which we live, we gently remind them of the importance of being accountable.

Modeling accountability also means adopting an attitude of humility that allows our teens to see us as human beings. We must let them see us make mistakes. It is oftentimes a fear of failure that frightens teens away from taking accountability for their actions. When they see that we, too, fail, but that we can admit our mistakes and make amends, they begin to understand that it's okay to fail. They understand that success can grow when you acknowledge failure.

It is equally important to praise our teens' successes. When a teen in our charge meets our expectations, is responsible and makes good choices, we should celebrate. With a smile and a little positive reinforcement, teens learn that responsible behavior is a good thing.

As we model what it looks like to be responsible, accountable adults, our teens will learn from the examples we set. They will learn how to be productive members of society who contribute in meaningful ways. And perhaps, most importantly, we can watch them flourish under this newfound sense of accountability. We will watch as they develop strength, courage and character. We will see them bloom with a self-confidence and self-respect that comes with maturity.

Play Fair

When we work with teens, we must be careful to be fair, a concept to which teens are much attuned. They are watching to see that we are objective and rational. When they evaluate our actions as being fair, they respond. If they feel treated unjustly, they rebel, seeing our efforts to establish rules and consequences as an attempt to oppress their burgeoning sense of independence.

Setting forth a list of rules and regulations, without helping teens see that they are indeed fair and just, leaves teens sensing a lack of control, a state they respond to by denying responsibility for their behavior. When kids feel that they have no control over their environment, they become angry and place blame. They come to resent rather than to be a part of the environment.

Expecting the Best

Along with working to create an overall environment of accountability, we must set forth clear expectations. Young people struggle to know right from wrong. They question what they can get away with and what they can't. It is with firm and clear expectations that they learn right from wrong and to take responsibility for their behavior.

Understand that teens do not view the world the same way that adults do. Sometimes they don't want to. Other times, they simply don't. Telling a teen he must clean up after himself doesn't necessarily mean he will fulfill your expectation. Telling him to clean the kitchen is telling him to clean the kitchen according to his definition of clean, which may mean putting the food away, but stacking the dishes in the sink and leaving crumbs on the counter. Being specific means clearly articulating your definition of clean, such as, *"Put the food away, wash and put away the dishes, wipe off the counters and rinse out the sink."*

Being vague or general in your expectations sets you both up for failure. You must be specific in your language, explaining precisely what you expect. If you don't, teens may sincerely think they have done what you've asked. They cleaned the kitchen. They will be confused and resentful when you indicate that they did not fulfill your expectation.

Raise Your Expectations

Sometimes we make the mistake of expecting too little. People in general rise to the level that is expected of them, and teens are no different. When we raise our expectations, we are in essence saying, "This is what I expect of you because this is what I know you can do. You are strong and mature and capable."

A mom shared a story that she successfully raised two boys with one sentence: "That's not who we are." There was undoubtedly more to itthan that, but her point was that she set forth an expectation for her children. Whenever a behavior or an attitude came into question, she clearly reminded them of the expectations for "who" they were. There was an expectation of decency in that home and the children rose to meet it.

Many adults who work with teens express surprise that teens, when given the chance, can be very good at governing themselves. Consider giving the teens with whom you work an opportunity to create their expectations for themselves. Have them outline their own boundaries. You might be surprised at how much they choose to expect of themselves.

Allowing kids the chance to determine what is right and wrong for themselves is a powerful way to teach them responsibility. These are the behaviors they find important. These are the boundaries they set for themselves based on their own values. Allowing teens this kind of freedom in setting expectations gives them ownership. It allows them to learn who they are and who they want to become. It also shows them that you trust them to do what is right.

Paying the Price

A big part of developing accountability is being consciously aware of the choices we make and the natural consequences of those choices. Setting out well-defined consequences for inappropriate behavior is an important part of helping teens learn to be accountable. When a teen makes a poor choice, and suffers the logically resulting consequences, he or she becomes aware that every action has an outcome.

If, for example, one of your expectations is successful performance in school, the consequence of not performing well is most effective when tied naturally to poor performance. Not being allowed to participate in after-school activities is a natural consequence of not doing well in class. After-school activities, after all, are considered extra-curricular. They are designed to come after the work of school is done. Not doing the work in school results in not being a part of what comes later. Another natural consequence might behaving to skip spending time with friends after school. Just as adults must do their job to enjoy a certain lifestyle, teens must do their job well, which is to be successful in school, before they can enjoy being with their friends.

Helping teens to see the natural outgrowth of their choices helps them to understand that their behavior creates results and that they are responsible for both.

Be Specific

Just as you work to be precise in outlining expectations, you must be equally precise in detailing consequences. You cannot assume that teens have an innate ability to recognize the consequences of their actions. They often do not. Telling an unmotivated teenager that poor performance in school will cause him trouble in the future will most likely fall on deaf ears. The future is a long way away for most teens. It is an indefinite, undetermined time in their lives. What matters to most teens is this moment right now.

Instead of presenting vague and indefinite consequences, be specific in setting out the results of certain behaviors. If they get a speeding ticket, they'll be riding the bus. If they talk back, they'll lose the cell phone. These types of specific consequences help teens learn that there are rules we must all follow. Life is easier if we follow the rules.

Being firm and specific in doling out consequences goes a long way in helping teens develop a sense of accountability. You'll find that your teens will start to follow the rules even when they obviously don't want to. They'll come to understand that no matter what else they do or say, they will be held responsible for the choices they make. They will learn to think before they act and to be responsible for those choices.

Be Consistent

It is essential to be consistent and follow through on whatever consequences have been set forth. By doing so, you are being honest and trustworthy. You are again modeling accountability by keeping a promise you made. When a teen has made an unacceptable choice, you must be sure he pays the price. Teens will learn which choices are appropriate as they find themselves consistently facing the consequences of their behavior. It is these learning experiences that help them understand what is and what is not responsible behavior.

Although remaining consistent can be difficult, changing the rules or making them up as you go is one of the worst things you can do. We are ruled by a harried existence. Sometimes we don't have time for follow through. However, we must slow down and prioritize these lessons in accountability. When kids are consistently held accountable for their behavior, they'll begin to get it. Having consistent rules and expectations and then holding yourself and your teens accountable is one of the greatest gifts you can give.

Remaining consistent can also be difficult

because kids are really good at arguing. They are far better at it than we are. However, you mustn't engage in a power struggle over previously stated consequences. Engaging in an argument sends the message that being accountable is up for debate. It isn't. It is an expectation. If you become worn down by their arguments and give in, they will see your lack of consistency as more chaos in a world they knew made no sense anyway.

Practice Makes Perfect

Learning to do anything well takes practice. Talking to your teens about how they can follow the rules and take responsibility for a behavior is an effective teaching technique. Have regular conversations with your teens about how they are doing. Help them brainstorm ways they can react to difficult situations in an appropriate manner, which will help them be more accountable when difficulties arise. They will truly understand that you have their best interests at heart. They will trust you with their struggles.

We must let teens practice taking responsibility for their actions, which means allowing them to make mistakes. We mustn't rush in to rescue them when life becomes difficult. Instead, we must allow them to be uncomfortable or even unhappy as a result of their choices. When we immediately race in to fix things, we limit their ability to take responsibility for themselves. We limit their ability to learn from their mistakes.

Celebrate the Growing Pains

Those who choose to work with kids often find it difficult to see them suffer. But suffering is a part of life. No one becomes who they are meant to be without experiencing a few growing pains along the way. We must allow teens to feel the resulting discomfort of their poor choices and then give them a means to cope. If we equip our teens with critical and analytical problem-solving skills, we give them the necessary tools to cope with disappointment and hardships. In this way, we prepare them to become functioning, responsible members of society.

If you can view letting kids experience failure and suffering the consequences of poor choices as a form of practice, you will be less likely to insist on protecting them from the necessary learning process. Practicing failure is a way for teens to learn that they won't always succeed, and that's okay. They don't have to make excuses. And they certainly shouldn't stop trying. We all fail and that's okay. We all make mistakes. We learn to cope in positive, healthy ways when we take responsibility for those mistakes.

A Future of Hope

We were all young once. We all had to learn, some of us the hard way, that we must be held accountable for our actions if we are to have and do and be all that we were designed for. We are now in the position to help our youth learn these same lessons. After all, and although it's a cliché, our future does indeed lie with the teens of today.

As we work with teens, we must be ever mindful that we are helping them grow and guiding them in their development. We mustn't simply expect. With a firm but gentle hand, we must teach. They will talk to us if we communicate openly and honestly, if we express our sincere desire to help them grow. And when they do, we must not be overly critical. They will make mistakes in their thinking and their behavior. Rather than condemning them, we must help them find ways to correct their thinking and behavior and make better choices in the future.

As we continue this journey with our teens, perhaps most importantly, we need to keep our sense of humor. The teenage years can be trying, not only for those who work with teens, but for the teens themselves. If you can laugh at yourself, if you can laugh at the world through the silly eyes of a teenager, you'll be well on your way to establishing trust. And it is trust, my friends, that creates the pure and giving environment in which you will be most effective in guiding the teens you love toward success.

Chapter 5 Questions for Reflection/Discussion

1. You discover a piece of equipment missing from the group room and suspect a certain teen of taking it. When you call attention to the fact that it's gone, no one comes forth with information. What options might you use to resolve this issue?

2. A teen comes to you and expresses concern about the choices another teen in the group is making. He swears you to secrecy. What would you do?

3. You are aware that a teenager in your group is having major difficulty at home with a step-parent. However, he refuses to talk about it. One day during group time he explodes with anger, gets into his car and drives away. How would you handle this situation, keeping in mind there are two sides to the story that the teen is living through?

4. You have set forth what you see as reasonable

expectations for behavior for a group outing. You are astonished when several of your teens begin a group assault, arguing that the rules you've outlined are ridiculous. They insist the rules you believe to be necessary are too rigid and need to be changed. What would you do to maintain your authority while also trying to help the group feel heard?

Relational Youth Ministry

I firmly believe that every teenager needs positive adult models in their lives just like yourself to help them navigate the challenges and issues of life. Every teenager I have ever met wants to be known, loved and cared for. All of these things are possible and can be realized in a young person's life over time. The relationships you cultivate with the youth you are entrusted to will impact their lives, and yours too, in ways that will last a lifetime.

Made in the USA
Columbia, SC
20 June 2018